✦ ✦ ✦ **SELLING THE MILL CITY** ✦ ✦ ✦

A Postcard Book

Minnesota Historical Society Press

www.mnhs.org/mhspress

Manufactured in China

10 9 8 7 6 5 4 3 2 1

International Standard Book Number 0-87351-460-2

From the collections of the Minnesota Historical Society

From 1880 to 1930, Minneapolis was the nation's Mill City. Flour milling companies knew they had a superior product, and they spent thousands of dollars to convince consumers that their flour was the best. From behemoths like Washburn-Crosby and Pillsbury to smaller mills that remained in business for only a few months or a few years, advertising cards, trade cards, and posters flooded businesses and homes. Some focused on the scientific aspects of their flour by advertising "uniform, strong gluten" that "builds strong bodies." Others inspired bakers with classical or renaissance scenes, reproduced in glorious color. Still others drew their names or their advertising gimmicks from U.S. history, calling on consumers' patriotism as they selected flour for use in their recipes. All of these advertisements were singular in their goal: selling the Mill City.

✦ ✦ ✦ **SELLING THE MILL CITY** ✦ ✦ ✦

Washburn's Superlative Flour
Washburn-Crosby Company, Minneapolis, Minnesota

Minnesota Historical Society Press ✦ ✦ ✦ http://www.mnhs.org/mhspress/

ON Christmas Night, 1776, Washington, with a ragged but valiant little army, crossed the Delaware river in a snow storm, at Trenton, N. J., fell upon and whipped the enemy, who, in his assumed security, was celebrating his triumph--A courageous incident in our country's fight for Freedom

and today

FREEDOM FLOUR
ATKINSON MILLING COMPANY, Minneapolis, Minn.

Freedom Flour
Atkinson Milling Company, Minneapolis, Minnesota

Minnesota Historical Society Press ✦ ✦ ✦ http://www.mnhs.org/mhspress/

Seal of Minnesota Flour
International Milling Company, Minneapolis, Minnesota

Minnesota Historical Society Press + + + http://www.mnhs.org/mhspress/

USE
FIRST-CLASS
POSTAGE

Eventually

Why Not Now?

✦ ✦ ✦ SELLING THE MILL CITY ✦ ✦ ✦

Gold Medal Flour (1922)

Washburn-Crosby Company, Minneapolis, Minnesota

Minnesota Historical Society Press ✦ ✦ ✦ http://www.mnhs.org/mhspress/

Diamond Medal Trade Mark Flour (1890–91)
Minneapolis Flour Manufacturing Company
Minneapolis, Minnesota

Minnesota Historical Society Press ✦ ✦ ✦ http://www.mnhs.org/mhspress/

Way Ahead!
N.W. SPECIAL
FLOUR

UNIFORM
STRONG
GLUTEN

SPRING PATENT
Atkinson's
N.W.
SPECIAL
FLOUR
MADE IN
Minneapolis

ATKINSON MILLING CO.
MINNEAPOLIS, MINN.

A Mill for Bakers

ATKINSON MILLING CO.
MINNEAPOLIS

N. W. Special Flour

Atkinson Milling Company, Minneapolis, Minnesota

Minnesota Historical Society Press + + + http://www.mnhs.org/mhspress/

Helping teach America to

Gold Medal Flour (1923)
Washburn-Crosby Company, Minneapolis, Minnesota

Minnesota Historical Society Press ✦ ✦ ✦ http://www.mnhs.org/mhspress/

Galaxy Roller Mills
Galaxy Mill Company, Minneapolis, Minnesota

Minnesota Historical Society Press + + + http://www.mnhs.org/mhspress/

Crown Roller Mill,
Christian Bro's Mill Co.
Minneapolis, Minn.

Without exception the BEST FLOUR made

For Sale by

✦ ✦ ✦ SELLING THE MILL CITY ✦ ✦ ✦

Crown Roller Mill

Christian Brothers Mill Company, Minneapolis, Minnesota

Minnesota Historical Society Press ✦ ✦ ✦ http://www.mnhs.org/mhspress/

The Table of the Fussy Husband.

A Husband who thought his Mother was the only Cook in the family, decided to take his Wife to the Mother's house that she might learn how to make Bread. The wife before leaving home secretly made a Loaf, using Washburn-Crosby's Gold Medal Flour, and hiding it in her trunk, placed it on the Mother's Table when no one was looking. At supper the Husband, upon eating some of the Loaf exclaimed "Mother, your bread is even better than it used to be!"

Moral:—Use

GOLD MEDAL FLOUR

For sale by.

E. B. Smith.

Gold Medal Flour
Washburn-Crosby Company, Minneapolis, Minnesota

Minnesota Historical Society Press + + + http://www.mnhs.org/mhspress/

50 LBS.

V&W

A REAL OLDE FASHIONED FLOUR

OF HAPPINESS

W.J. JENNISON CO.

50 YEARS

WARRANTED
APPLETON.MINN.

Golden Wedding

Highest Patent

W.J. JENNISON CO.
GENERAL OFFICES
MINNEAPOLIS, MINN.

BLEACHED

Minnesota Historical Society Press + + + http://www.mnhs.org/mhspress/

Ben-Hur FLOUR

Royal Milling Co.
PERFECT PATENT FLOUR.

MINNEAPOLIS MILL,
CAPACITY, 2,500 BBLS.

ROYAL MILL,
CAPACITY, 500 BBLS.

Minneapolis, Minn.

Ben-Hur Flour (1906)
Royal Milling Company, Minneapolis, Minnesota

Minnesota Historical Society Press + + + http://www.mnhs.org/mhspress/

Eventually

WASHBURN-CROSBY'S GOLD MEDAL FLOUR

Why Not Now?

Gold Medal Flour
Washburn-Crosby Company, Minneapolis, Minnesota

Minnesota Historical Society Press ✦ ✦ ✦ http://www.mnhs.org/mhspress/

TESTED WHEAT

makes uniformity in our

Seal of Minnesota Flour

NEW PRAGUE FLOURING MILL

Seal of Minnesota Flour

Assures Results

The flour he uses can make or break a baker.

You bakers who read this know that this is a fact.

Therefore, we know that you will agree that when we tell you that

Seal of Minnesota "assures" results, it is a strong statement.

We wouldn't dare make this statement unless we were willing to stand behind it. We *are* willing. Make us prove it. Will you?

NEW PRAGUE FLOURING MILL   NEW PRAGUE, MINNESOTA

Seal of Minnesota Flour (1923)
New Prague Flouring Mill, New Prague, Minnesota

Minnesota Historical Society Press + + + http://www.mnhs.org/mhspress/

Daniel Webster

DANIEL WEBSTER

FLOUR
EAGLE ROLLER MILL CO.
NEW ULM, MINN.

for Better Baking

Daniel Webster Flour
Eagle Roller Mill Company, New Ulm, Minnesota

Minnesota Historical Society Press + + + http://www.mnhs.org/mhspress/

Conscientious effort to
maintain Gold Medal Flour
at a standard to justify the
pride that Minneapolis has
for it is the unvarying policy
of the

WASHBURN-CROSBY
COMPANY

Gothic Design—Lower tracery is in the manner of a door of a little French shrine XV° Century. The lion is the symbol familiar to designers of all ages—the Christian symbol of the Redeemer.

Gold Medal Flour (1924–25)
Washburn-Crosby Company, Minneapolis, Minnesota

Minnesota Historical Society Press + + + http://www.mnhs.org/mhspress/

4 APPLE BLOSSOMS. Kenyon

COPYRIGHT 1910 BY THE GERLACH-BARKLOW CO., JOLIET, ILL., U.S.A.

PURITY   CLEANLINESS   QUALITY

ARDEE FLOUR

MANUFACTURED BY

HUBBARD MILLING COMPANY

MANKATO, MINNESOTA

1912		April		1912		
SUN	MON	TUES	WED	THUR	FRI	SAT
..	1	2	3	4	5	6
7	8	9	10	11	12	13
14	15	16	17	18	19	20
21	22	23	24	25	26	27
28	29	30	..	..	..	..

Ardee Flour (1912)
Hubbard Milling Company, Mankato, Minnesota

Minnesota Historical Society Press + + + http://www.mnhs.org/mhspress/

ROBIN HOOD FLOUR

"FROM NOW ON"

ROBIN HOOD FLOUR

INTERNATIONAL MILLING CO.

ROBIN HOOD FLOUR

FREE ALUMINUM PREMIUMS

QUARTER COUPON INSIDE

Robin Hood Flour
International Milling Company, Minneapolis, Minnesota

Minnesota Historical Society Press + + + http://www.mnhs.org/mhspress/

Minnesota Historical Society Press + + + http://www.mnhs.org/mhspress/

Robin Hood Flour
International Milling Company, Minneapolis, Minnesota

Minnesota Historical Society Press + + + http://www.mnhs.org/mhspress/

Ethan Allen Flour
Wells Flour Milling Company (location unknown)

Minnesota Historical Society Press + + + http://www.mnhs.org/mhspress/

I'LL MAKE ASSURANCE DOUBLE SURE

SHAKESPEARE

Eventually

Why
Not
Now
?

WASHBURN-CROSBY CO.

+ + + **SELLING THE MILL CITY** + + +

Gold Medal Flour

Washburn-Crosby Company, Minneapolis, Minnesota

Minnesota Historical Society Press + + + http://www.mnhs.org/mhspress/

The Occident Girl Says –

Occident Flour

Makes More and
Better Bread
— Thats Economy

OCCIDENT
FLOUR

Costs More–Worth It

Minnesota Historical Society Press + + + http://www.mnhs.org/mhspress/

The Queen of "Flours"

PRMA DNNA
ANCHOR M__ COMPANY
TRADE MARK
PATENT U.S.A.
SUPERIOR

Prima Donna Flour
Anchor Mill Company, Superior, Wisconsin

Minnesota Historical Society Press + + + http://www.mnhs.org/mhspress/

Washburn's Best Flour (1889)
Washburn Mill Company, Minneapolis, Minnesota

Minnesota Historical Society Press ✦ ✦ ✦ http://www.mnhs.org/mhspress/

USE
FIRST-CLASS
POSTAGE

TELEPHONE

An extra high grade spring wheat
flour for particular trade.
We Guarantee it absolutely.

CANNON VALLEY MILLING CO.

OFFICES-822-823 FLOUR EXCHANGE

MINNEAPOLIS,   **MINN.**

Made in our new all water power Mill at Cannon Falls, Minn.   Daily Capacity 1500 barrels.

Telephone Flour
Cannon Valley Milling Company, Minneapolis, Minnesota

Minnesota Historical Society Press + + + http://www.mnhs.org/mhspress/

USE
FIRST-CLASS
POSTAGE

Gold Medal Flour
Washburn-Crosby Company, Minneapolis, Minnesota

Minnesota Historical Society Press + + + http://www.mnhs.org/mhspress/

USE
FIRST-CLASS
POSTAGE

Chas. A. Pillsbury & Co.

· Merchant Millers ·
Minneapolis, Minn.
· U·S·A ·

America's Finest

Pillsbury's
BEST
XXXX
Minneapolis, Minn.

Daily Capacity
10,500
Barrels

Geo. A. Pillsbury
John S. Pillsbury
Chas. A. Pillsbury
Fred C. Pillsbury

Pillsbury Mills, Minneapolis, Minn. U.S.A.

FOR SALE HERE

Pillsbury's Best Flour (1890)
Charles A. Pillsbury and Company, Minneapolis, Minnesota

Minnesota Historical Society Press + + + http://www.mnhs.org/mhspress/

USE
FIRST-CLASS
POSTAGE

Minnesota Girl

MINNESOTA GIRL

FANCY PATENT
FLOUR
BLEACHED
MILLED BY
CAPITAL FLOUR MILLS, INC.
ST. PAUL, MINN.

Our Guarantee

M INNESOTA GIRL FLOUR is guaranteed to be a pure, sweet and sound flour, and to give satisfaction, or we will refund the full purchase price.

This flour is specially milled from a combination of hard spring wheats accurately blended to produce a high grade patent flour specially adapted for home baking.

Minnesota Girl Flour
Capital Flour Mills, Inc., St. Paul, Minnesota

Minnesota Historical Society Press + + + http://www.mnhs.org/mhspress/

✦ ✦ ✦ SELLING THE MILL CITY ✦ ✦ ✦

Gold Medal Flour (1920–21)
Washburn-Crosby Company, Minneapolis, Minnesota

Minnesota Historical Society Press ✦ ✦ ✦ http://www.mnhs.org/mhspress/

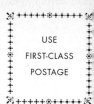

USE

FIRST-CLASS

POSTAGE